Pebble Plus

Women in Sports

DANICA PATRICK

by Abby Colich

Peachtree

CAPSTONE PRESS
a capstone imprint

Pebble Plus is published by Capstone Press
1710 Roe Crest Drive, North Mankato, Minnesota 56003
www.mycapstone.com

Library of Congress Cataloging-in-Publication Data
Cataloging-in-Publication Data is on file with the Library of Congress.
ISBN 978-1-4914-7971-1 (library binding)
ISBN 978-1-4914-8567-5 (paperback)
ISBN 978-1-4914-8573-6 (eBook PDF)

Editorial Credits
Abby Colich, editor; Sarah Bennett, designer; Eric Gohl, media researcher;
Katy LaVigne, production specialist

Photo Credits
Dreamstime: Jabberjaw, 15; Getty Images: Jonathan Ferrey, 7, 13; Newscom: Icon SMI/David J.
Griffin, 17, Icon SMI/Mark Cowan, 11, MCT/Jeff Siner, 19, Reuters/USA/Stringer, 9; Shutterstock:
Action Sports Photography, 5, Aepsilon, 2, 24, Daniel Huerlimann-BEELDE, cover (all), 1, 11
(background), 21, 22, Vladru, 3, 23

Note to Parents and Teachers

The Women in Sports set supports national curriculum standards for social studies
related to people, places, and culture. This book describes and illustrates Danica
Patrick. The images support early readers in understanding the text. The repetition
of words and phrases helps early readers learn new words. This book also introduces
early readers to subject-specific vocabulary words, which are defined in the Glossary
section. Early readers may need assistance to read some words and to use the Table of
Contents, Glossary, Read More, Internet Sites, Critical Thinking Using the Common
Core, and Index sections of the book.

Printed in the United States of America in North Mankato, Minnesota.
092015 009221CGS16

Table of Contents

A Born Racer

Danica Patrick was born March 25, 1982. She grew up in Roscoe, Illinois. Her father raced snowmobiles. Danica and her sister, Brooke, raced go-karts.

TIMELINE

1982
born near
Roscoe, Illinois

1992
begins racing
go-karts

Danica moved to England
when she was 16. She raced
in the Formula series. The races
made her a better driver.
In 2002 she came back
to the United States.

TIMELINE

1982	1992	1998	2002
born near Roscoe, Illinois	begins racing go-karts	moves to England	returns to racing in the United States

An INDYCAR Star

Danica joined INDYCAR in 2005.

It was an exciting year.

She came in fourth place

at the Indianapolis 500.

She was Rookie of the Year.

TIMELINE

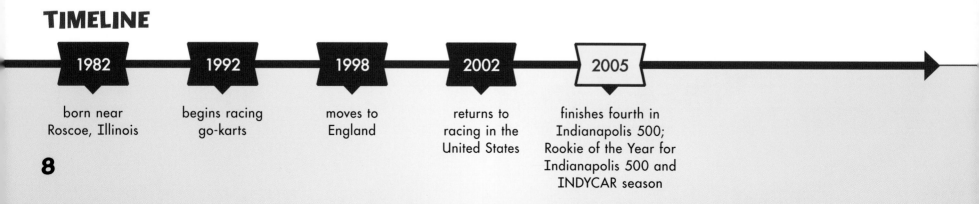

1982	1992	1998	2002	2005
born near Roscoe, Illinois	begins racing go-karts	moves to England	returns to racing in the United States	finishes fourth in Indianapolis 500; Rookie of the Year for Indianapolis 500 and INDYCAR season

At the 2006 Indianapolis 500,

Danica also did well.

She finished in eighth place.

That year she had

eight top-10 finishes.

TIMELINE

1982	1992	1998	2002	2005	2006
born near Roscoe, Illinois	begins racing go-karts	moves to England	returns to racing in the United States	finishes fourth in Indianapolis 500; Rookie of the Year for Indianapolis 500 and INDYCAR season	finishes eighth at the Indianapolis 500

Danica drives car number 16.

Danica won the Indy Japan 300 in 2008. She was the first woman to win an INDYCAR race. She finished third at the 2009 Indianapolis 500. This was the highest ever by a woman.

TIMELINE

1982	1992	1998	2002	2005	2006
born near Roscoe, Illinois	begins racing go-karts	moves to England	returns to racing in the United States	finishes fourth in Indianapolis 500; Rookie of the Year for Indianapolis 500 and INDYCAR season	finishes eighth at the Indianapolis 500

2008

wins the Indy
Japan 300

2009

finishes third
in the
Indianapolis 500

Danica finished 33 INDYCAR

races in a row in 2010.

That was a record for women

and men. She had eight top-10

finishes. In 2011 Danica began

racing NASCAR part time.

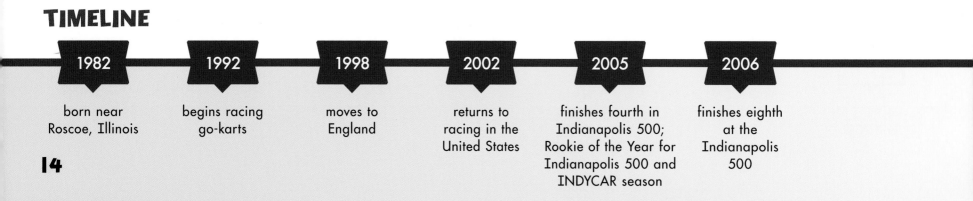

TIMELINE

1982	1992	1998	2002	2005	2006
born near Roscoe, Illinois	begins racing go-karts	moves to England	returns to racing in the United States	finishes fourth in Indianapolis 500; Rookie of the Year for Indianapolis 500 and INDYCAR season	finishes eighth at the Indianapolis 500

2008	2009	2010	2011
wins the Indy Japan 300	finishes third in the Indianapolis 500	finishes 33 races in a row	begins racing NASCAR part time

A NASCAR Career

Danica began NASCAR racing full time in 2012. It did not start well. She was in several crashes. She did not place high in most races.

TIMELINE

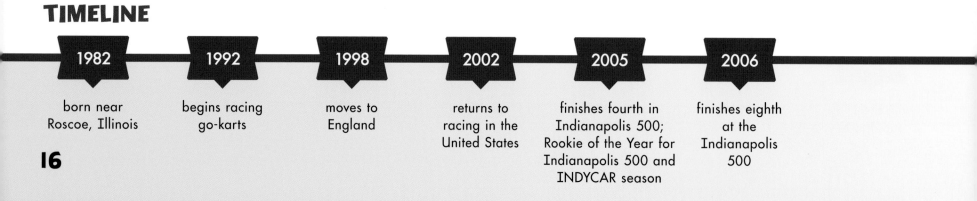

1982	1992	1998	2002	2005	2006
born near Roscoe, Illinois	begins racing go-karts	moves to England	returns to racing in the United States	finishes fourth in Indianapolis 500; Rookie of the Year for Indianapolis 500 and INDYCAR season	finishes eighth at the Indianapolis 500

2008	2009	2010	2011	2012
wins the Indy Japan 300	finishes third in the Indianapolis 500	finishes 33 races in a row	begins racing NASCAR part time	begins NASCAR racing full time

Things got better in 2013.
Danica won the pole position
for the Daytona 500. She led
the race for several laps.
She finished in eighth place.

TIMELINE

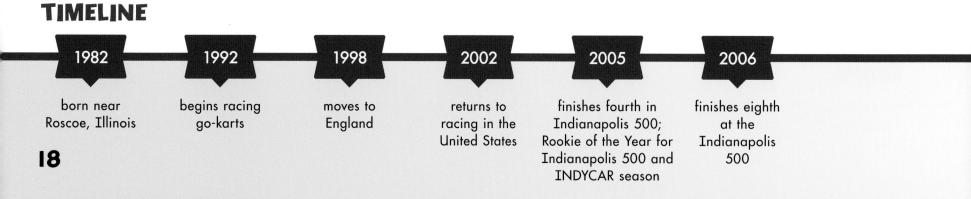

1982	1992	1998	2002	2005	2006
born near Roscoe, Illinois	begins racing go-karts	moves to England	returns to racing in the United States	finishes fourth in Indianapolis 500; Rookie of the Year for Indianapolis 500 and INDYCAR season	finishes eighth at the Indianapolis 500

2008	2009	2010	2011	2012	2013
wins the Indy Japan 300	finishes third in the Indianapolis 500	finishes 33 races in a row	begins racing NASCAR part time	begins NASCAR racing full time	wins the Daytona 500 pole position; takes eighth place in the race

In 2015 Danica broke a record for top-10 finishes by a woman in the Sprint Cup Series. Danica is leading the way for female race car drivers.

TIMELINE

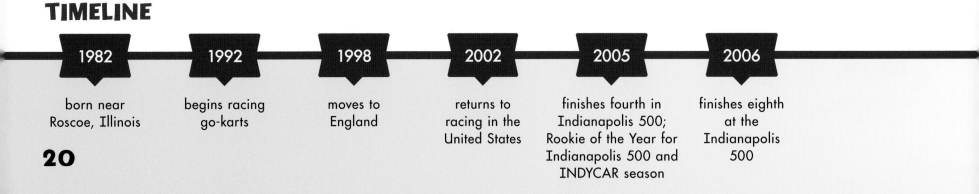

1982	1992	1998	2002	2005	2006
born near Roscoe, Illinois	begins racing go-karts	moves to England	returns to racing in the United States	finishes fourth in Indianapolis 500; Rookie of the Year for Indianapolis 500 and INDYCAR season	finishes eighth at the Indianapolis 500

2008	2009	2010	2011	2012	2013	2015
wins the Indy Japan 300	finishes third in the Indianapolis 500	finishes 33 races in a row	begins racing NASCAR part time	begins NASCAR racing full time	wins the Daytona 500 pole position; takes eighth place in the race	breaks record for most top-10 finishes by a female

Glossary

Formula series—a race car league in Europe

INDYCAR—a racing league in North America in which drivers use Indy Cars

NASCAR—a racing league in North America and Europe in which drivers use stock cars

pole position—the inside spot in the front row of cars at the beginning of a race

record—when something is done better than anyone has ever done it before

rookie—a first-year player or participant

season—the time of year in which a sport takes place

series—a group of related things or events that come one after another

Read More

Jameson, Anderson. *Danica Patrick.* Awesome Athletes. Minneapolis, Minn.: Checkerboard Library, 2015.

Miller, Connie Colwell. *Danica Patrick.* NASCAR Heroes. Minneapolis, Minn.: ABDO Publishing, 2013.

Pratt, Laura. *Danica Patrick.* Remarkable People. New York: AV2 by Weigl, 2013.

Internet Sites

FactHound offers a safe, fun way to find Internet sites related to this book. All of the sites on FactHound have been researched by our staff.

Here's all you do:
Visit *www.facthound.com*
Type in this code: 9781491479711

 **Super-cool stuff!** Check out projects, games and lots more at **www.capstonekids.com**

Critical Thinking Using the Common Core

1. Danica raced go-karts as a child. How might this have prepared her for a career as a race car driver? (Integration of Knowledge and Ideas)

2. Reread the text on page 12. Then look at the photograph on page 13. What is Danica holding? (Craft and Structure)

Index